Promoting Sustainable Behaviour

A practical guide to what works

T0298905

Adam Corner

Head of Talking Climate Programme,
The Climate Outreach and Information Network (COIN),
Old Music Hall, 106–108 Cowley Road,
Oxford OX4 1JE, United Kingdom.
Email: adam@coinet.org.uk
Web: www.coinet.org.uk

Climate Outreach and Information Network is a charity established in 2004, dedicated to helping people communicate climate change more effectively.

First published in 2012 by Dō Sustainability
87 Lonsdale Road, Oxford OX2 7ET, UK

ISBN 978-1-909293-13-7 (eBook-ePub)
ISBN 978-1-909293-14-4 (eBook-PDF)
ISBN 978-1-909293-12-0 (Paperback)

A catalogue record for this title is available from the British Library.

At Dō Sustainability we strive to minimize our environmental impacts and carbon footprint through reducing waste, recycling and offsetting our CO_2 emissions, including those created through publication of this book. For more information on our environmental policy see **www.dosustainability.com**.

Page design and typesetting by Alison Rayner
Cover by Becky Chilcott

For further information on Dō Sustainability, visit our website:
www.dosustainability.com

DōShorts

Dō Sustainability is the publisher of DōShorts: short, high-value ebooks that distil sustainability best practice and business insights for busy, results-driven professionals. Each DōShort can be read in 90 minutes.

New and forthcoming DōShorts -- stay up to date

We publish 3 to 5 new DōShorts each month. The best way to keep up to date? Sign up to our short, monthly newsletter. Go to **www.dosustainability.com/newsletter** to sign up to the Dō Newsletter. Some of our latest and forthcoming titles include:

- *Green Jujitsu: Embed Sustainability into Your Organisation* Gareth Kane
- *How to Make your Company a Recognised Sustainability Champion* Brendan May
- *Making the Most of Standards* Adrian Henriques
- *Promoting Sustainable Behaviour: A Practical Guide to What Works* Adam Corner
- *Solar Photovoltaics Business Briefing* David Thorpe
- *Sustainability in the Public Sector* Sonja Powell
- *Sustainability Reporting for SMEs* Elaine Cohen
- *Sustainable Transport Fuels Business Briefing* David Thorpe
- *The Changing Profile of Corporate Climate Change Risk* Mark Trexler & Laura Kosloff
- *The First 100 Days: Plan, Prioritise & Build a Sustainable Organisation* Anne Augustine
- *The Short Guide to SRI* Cary Krosinsky

Subscriptions

In additional to individual sales and rentals, we offer organisational subscriptions to our full collection of published and forthcoming books. To discuss a subscription for your organisation, email **veruschka@dosustainability.com**

Write for us, or suggest a DōShort

Please visit **www.dosustainability.com** for our full publishing programme. If you don't find what you need, write for us! Or Suggest a DōShort on our website. We look forward to hearing from you.

....

Abstract

PROMOTING SUSTAINABLE BEHAVIOUR is a critical part of society's response to climate change. The aim of this short and practically focused book is to show how to make the most of campaigns to promote sustainable behaviour – in households, when commuting, in the workplace and beyond. There are more and less effective ways of encouraging people to act in a more sustainable way, and some important pitfalls to avoid. But by summarising 'what works' and pulling out the most important take-home messages, this book contains the tools for maximising the success of any sustainable behaviour initiative. By looking beyond individual behaviours and thinking more about people's identities and values; by considering the social signals that provide such important cues for our everyday behaviour; by using the best strategies to attract (and keep) people's interest; and by understanding how to break bad habits and create good ones, this guide to promoting sustainable behaviour offers the best chance of making a sustainable behaviour campaign work.

About The Author

 **DR ADAM CORNER** is a researcher and writer whose work focuses on the psychology of communicating climate change. He leads the Talking Climate programme for the Climate Outreach and Information Network (a charity which specialises in climate change communication), and is a Research Associate in the School of Psychology at Cardiff University, UK. He has published widely in leading academic journals, writes regularly for the *Guardian* newspaper and other national media, and edits the website 'Talking Climate' (**www.talkingclimate.org**), the gateway to research on climate change communication.

Adam's work aims to bridge the gap between academic research and the range of groups – policy-makers, practitioners, businesses and community groups – who can make best use of it.

....

Contents

How much of a difference can changes in individual behaviour make? Isn't climate change – and the challenge of sustainability more generally – just too big a problem for individuals and communities to worry about? Why focus on the behaviour of ordinary people when political agreements and technological advances will do more to tackle climate change than anything an individual could achieve?

The way that a message about sustainable behaviour is 'framed' (the language used, the associations that are triggered, and the reasons that are given for it) will have a big impact on how people respond to it. And different ways of framing a message speak to very different values. Understanding how to structure messages about sustainable behaviour so that they have the biggest impact in the long term is the aim of this chapter.

CHAPTER 1

Promoting Sustainable Behaviour: What's The Point?

HOW MUCH OF A DIFFERENCE can changes in individual behaviour make? Isn't climate change – and the challenge of sustainability more generally – just too big a problem for individuals and communities to worry about? Why focus on the behaviour of ordinary people when political agreements and technological advances will do more to tackle climate change than anything an individual could achieve?

These are all critical questions for anyone interested in promoting sustainable behaviour – whether at home or in the workplace – to ask themselves. After all, if it were possible to wave a magic low-carbon wand and solve climate change overnight through new technologies, the strict regulation of high-polluting industries, or a binding political agreement that all the world's countries signed up to, wouldn't that make more sense than focusing on everyday attitudes and behaviour?

The problem, of course, is that there is no magic low-carbon wand – but even if there were, it would be waved by a person as susceptible to the quirks, biases and pitfalls of human judgement as anyone else. While it is comforting to draw sharp distinctions between politics, technology and individuals, the reality is that human behaviour underpins it all. Political parties will not pass legislation that is patently unpopular among the electorate. Technological advances can provide low-carbon alternatives like electric buses, but a zero-emissions bus will have zero passengers unless people decide to use it. And even the most carefully planned policy interventions can backfire if they don't take account of how people – the wildcard in any equation – will respond.

For example, if a driver who replaces their car with a fuel-efficient model takes advantage of the cheaper running costs and drives further and more often, then the amount of carbon saved is clearly reduced. This is what's known as a 'rebound' effect – one of many pitfalls that plague well-intentioned campaigns to promote sustainable behaviour. Rebound effects like these – where people take two steps forward and one step back – occur because no single behaviour takes place in a vacuum.

Consider campaigns in other areas of life. If the end-result of a television advert to promote the use of seatbelts was that drivers felt safer and drove faster, the ad would only be considered a partial success. If a drive to end teenage obesity resulted in an increase in the number of adolescents with self-image problems and eating disorders, this undermines the value of the campaign. And sustainable behaviours are no different – they have to be seen as small parts of a bigger picture, not isolated and separated from their wider impacts.

Studies have found[1] that on average, only about two-thirds of the calculated carbon reductions for a given household action (e.g. lowering the thermostat or reducing food waste) are likely to be achieved in reality. This is because money saved on the heating bill is (potentially) money available for a flight abroad, or some other high-carbon activity.

Promoting sustainable behaviour is not necessarily as easy as it first appears, but this is where simple, easy-to-apply and practical advice about 'what works' comes in. The aim of this short and practically focused book is to show how to make the most of campaigns to promote sustainable behaviour – in households, when commuting, in the workplace and beyond.

Simple and painless?

Generating long-lasting and meaningful changes in sustainable behaviour is a huge challenge. When first confronted with this issue, many people assumed that the problem was simply a lack of information – that once people knew how environmentally damaging their actions were, they'd soon start making changes. Unfortunately, the 'pamphlet approach' to sustainable behaviour has only had limited effectiveness – public information campaigns need more than just a clever slogan and the right information in order to succeed.[2]

Many sustainability initiatives over the past half a decade have responded to this by targeting low-hanging fruit – so-called 'simple and painless' behaviour changes like unplugging phone chargers, switching to energy-saving light-bulbs, or re-using plastic bags. The idea – which makes intuitive sense – is that these simple changes provide a 'way in', and may act as a catalyst for more substantial changes (in terms of energy saved) in the future.

Unfortunately, there is only limited evidence that starting with simple and painless changes is necessarily the best way of catalysing further changes – and there is a risk that people will feel they have 'done their bit'.[3] As Box 1 shows, there is a huge difference in the carbon-saving impact of different behaviours, but seldom is this reflected in sustainable behaviour initiatives.

These examples illustrate an important point: that it is possible to 'do behaviour change' in better or worse ways. Focusing on activities that have only a tiny payoff in terms of energy use can only be justified if they are the first step on a ladder that leads to more significant energy savings, something that the evidence presented in this book can help with. If low-impact changes (including things like switching off a few lights around the office) become an end in themselves, then the effort expended is probably not worth it. But if a strategy for promoting sustainable behaviour is as evidence-based as possible, engages with people at a deeper level than single behaviours, and gives thought to how people's personal values and social identities shape a wide range of behaviours, then there are important – in fact, essential – gains to be made in terms of building a sustainable society.

Behaviour change matters

In both the private and public sectors, it is now widely accepted that reducing energy consumption is a key battleground for tackling carbon emissions. The UK government – although falling well short of its claim to be the 'greenest ever' – is pushing ahead with ambitious plans that should (if they are successful) see significant changes in energy use among householders. 'Smart' energy meters are gradually being rolled out, and the flagship 'Green Deal' aims to insulate millions of homes by 2020.

Installing wall or cavity insulation might seem like a good example of a change in people's living arrangements that is purely technical – something that doesn't require thinking about people's attitudes or behaviours. But as the sustainable behaviour specialists Alexa Spence and Nick Pidgeon from Cardiff University have argued,[4] changes in household insulation depend on some key assumptions. In particular, the overheating of residential buildings has to become socially unacceptable, and people will have to be motivated to make changes to their home heating routines if they are not to fall into the 'rebound' trap. These are behavioural issues, not technical ones.

So promoting sustainable behaviour matters and ensuring that any sustainable programme is based on the best available research and practical case studies is an essential piece of the puzzle. Many people are wary of committing themselves to changes in their personal behaviour when it seems as if bigger gains can be made elsewhere. But unless people can identify with and understand climate change and sustainability at a personal level, those political and technological shifts will simply never happen. It is not a choice between technologies, policies and changing behaviour – the transition to a sustainable, low-carbon society requires all three.

So this book is for anyone who wants to ensure that their sustainable behaviour campaign – in the workplace or beyond – stands the best chance of working, and doesn't fall victim to the traps into which too many well-intentioned sustainability initiatives fall.

Each of the following chapters focuses on a different aspect of promoting sustainable behaviour, and is designed with practical outcomes in mind. The structure of each chapter includes a quick-start, 'what you need to know' summary at the outset, plus a case study, essential background theory that holds it all together, and advice on how to put this theory into practice.

BOX 1: Sustainable behaviours – making the most impact

Something so often missing from conversations about sustainable behaviour is how different actions stack up against each other. Does it matter if everyone leaves their phone-chargers plugged in? Is it better to car-share or ride to work on a half-empty bus? And how many years would you have to buy low-carbon orange juice for before you saved the same amount of carbon as avoiding one return flight between Spain and the UK?*

This box sets out some well-known sustainable behaviours – colour-coded to show how much energy they are likely to save. Keeping information like this close at hand helps to make an intimidatingly complex problem more manageable: don't spend too much time worrying about phone-chargers if there's a chance of targeting something more significant.

It's important to keep a sense of proportion by focusing on the big wins. In an office, space heating and air conditioning are better targets than lighting and standby settings. It's also worth asking yourself whether you would like to be bugged about certain things – no-one really wants to be told how to make a cup of tea, and so although boiling the kettle more efficiently will save energy, it might also make enemies of the very people you want to reach. An eco-kettle that does the job for people might be more sensible in this case.

It's also worth busting some popular myths about energy-saving. In buildings, air conditioning is often the largest consumer of electricity. In an office, computers, printers and faxes will probably use far more electricity than lighting. Low energy bulbs do take half a minute to fully warm up, but they use no more energy during this time than they do when they are on. Although lighting is not the biggest drain on energy, it is worth turning them off – even for a short time – and it won't shorten their life either. About 2 kg of carbon is saved for every short journey that is made using a bike or on foot instead of a car. Switching to an energy-efficient light-bulb only saves 10 kg over a whole year – so getting to grips with your commuting can have a significant impact.

But if swapping a car journey for a bike ride is a good idea, then swapping a flight for a train journey is even better. London to Paris by Eurostar uses about 90% less carbon than taking a flight – and flying is by far and away the most energy-intensive way of travelling (unless you are partial to pan-European road trips in monster 4x4 trucks with no companions with whom to split your carbon footprint).

HIGH IMPACT

Avoiding a flight – or cutting it out altogether. A plane is almost always the most carbon-intensive way of travelling. European trains – unlike British ones – are mostly fast and reliable.

Cycling to work – an average car sitting in a traffic jam in rush hour wastes 100 kg of carbon over a week. Cycling is essentially carbon-free.

Insulating a loft/roof space – over 40 years an impressive 35 tonnes of carbon can be saved (about three years worth of the average British carbon footprint)

MEDIUM IMPACT

Computing equipment – older, slower, desktop machines use more power than energy-efficient laptops (which also tend to switch themselves off). But the biggest impact of computing equipment is in the production of it, not the electricity to run it. So buying new kit for the sake of it is not necessarily a good idea.

Lighting – low energy light-bulbs use around a fifth of the electricity old-fashioned ones. The more you replace, the more you save.

Laundry – washing clothes at lower temperatures (30 degrees) and drying them naturally uses about a sixth of the energy compared to high-temperature washes plus tumble drying. Over a year this adds up.

LOW IMPACT

Plastic bags – although there are good reasons to avoid unnecessary waste, the carbon impact of a plastic bag is minimal.

Mobile phone-chargers – there is no reason not to unplug them when not in use, and newer phones need charging more often and absorb a lot more power. But phone-chargers plugged in pale in comparison to TVs and other electrical equipment on standby.

SOURCES: 5,6

*Researchers from the Tyndall Centre calculated that you would have to make 32 years' worth of daily purchases of 'lower carbon' Tesco orange juice to save the same amount of carbon as avoiding just one return flight from the UK to Spain.

Box 1 is intended to give you a flavour of the relative impact of different actions that people can take around the home or on the move. But for more detailed information on the carbon savings of specific changes, use the Energy Saving Trust website, and the interactive tools and resources it contains: **http://www.energysavingtrust.org.uk/**.

....

CHAPTER 2

Framing Your Messages: What Values Are You Appealing To?

What you need to know

THE WAY THAT A MESSAGE about sustainable behaviour is 'framed' (the language used, the associations that are triggered, and the reasons that are given for it) will have a big impact on how people respond to it. And different ways of framing a message speak to very different values. Understanding how to structure messages about sustainable behaviour so that they have the biggest impact in the long term is the aim of this chapter.

A value is usually defined as a 'guiding principle in the life of a person'. Over several decades, and through research conducted in over 60 countries,[7] there is now a huge body of evidence that shows that certain values and beliefs tend to go together, while others tend to be opposed to each other. There are two broad categories of values, which are known as 'self-enhancing' and 'self-transcending'. People who identify strongly with 'self-enhancing' or 'extrinsic' values (e.g. materialism, personal ambition) tend not to identify strongly with 'self-transcending' or 'intrinsic' values (e.g. benevolence, respect for the environment).

There are some important practical implications to this research: people who hold 'self-transcendent' values (especially pro-environmental values and high levels of altruism) are more likely to engage in sustainable behaviour,[8] show higher concern about environmental risks like climate change,[9] are more likely to engage in specific sustainable behaviours such as recycling[10] and are more likely to support policies to tackle climate change.[11]

> *This means that unless campaigns to promote sustainable behaviour make an attempt to target 'self-transcending' values, they may inadvertently promote precisely the types of personal and cultural values that will make sustainable behaviour less likely in the longer term. And this is why the way that messages and campaigns are 'framed' is so important.*

Consider two different ways of encouraging people to car-share on the commute to work. One option would be to tell people how much money they will save on petrol. This would be a 'self-enhancing' reason for car-sharing – and there is no doubt that appealing to people's wallets may be an effective way of selling the idea of car-sharing to them. A second option would be to emphasise the environmental benefits of car-sharing. This would be a 'self-transcendent' reason for car-sharing because it does not (directly) benefit individuals. This may also be an effective way of encouraging people to car-share.

If the challenge of sustainability was simply to sign as many people up to car-sharing schemes as possible, then the choice would be simple: go with the one that is most effective. But of course, the challenge of sustainability is vastly more complex than this, which means that anyone seeking to promote sustainable behaviour has to ask 'what happens next?'

> *Research suggests that in order to create a situation where one behavioural change will lead to another, it is important to focus on self-transcending values and environmental reasons for sustainable behaviour.*

The key to promoting meaningful changes in sustainable behaviour – that do more than just pay lip service to tackling climate change – is to nurture and develop a sense of environmental identity or citizenship.[12,13] When a person acts for self-interested reasons, that person will perceive themselves as someone who does things for their own benefit. They will only engage in further sustainable behaviours if there is something in it for them – as soon as the 'sweeteners' dry up, so will their interest in sustainability.

But if people begin to think of themselves as 'someone who does things for the environment', the chance that they will engage in other sustainable behaviours is much higher. It may not always be the quickest way of promoting a specific sustainable behaviour, but ultimately people can figure out for themselves whether something is in their own interest or not. The job of a sustainable behaviour practitioner is to help them see the bigger picture, and make the arguments about sustainability that an appeal to their wallet cannot do.

If you only do one thing...

Think really carefully about how to ensure that promoting sustainable behaviour works in the long, as well as the short term. Make a list of all the possible reasons you can think of for engaging in a particular behaviour that you're interested in (e.g. encouraging car-sharing). Divide them into 'self-interested' and 'self-transcendent' groups, and before you reach for the money-saving lever, try to construct a *less self-serving way of framing your message.*

The theory that makes it work

One of the defining debates within the environmental movement over the past decade has been between those who believe that applying the techniques and strategies of marketing physical products is the best way of promoting sustainable behaviour (social marketing), and those who have argued that this approach – trying to 'sell' climate change – is ultimately counterproductive unless the right underlying values are targeted by campaigns, and unless the messages are 'framed' in a way that encourages sustainable behaviours across the board.

In some ways, this debate is less about the best way of achieving immediate changes in sustainable behaviour than it is about the best way of achieving sustained and consistent changes over a longer period of time. A recent study by researchers at Cardiff University[14] found that framing a sustainable behaviour – car-sharing – in two different ways had an impact on how likely people were to engage in other sustainable behaviours. In an experiment, some people were primed to think about the environmental benefits of car-sharing, while others were encouraged to think about financial reasons for this activity. The people who had considered environmental reasons for car-sharing were more likely to subsequently recycle, showing that the reasons given for one sustainable behaviour impact on the chance that people will engage in other sustainable behaviours in the future.

Intentionally or unintentionally, all information is 'framed' by the context in which it appears. This could mean the individual words and phrases that are used (sometimes called 'conceptual framing'), and is more akin to the 'spin' that is put on a message (like describing a product as containing 50% less fat, when in fact it still contains more fat than any of its competitors).

But framing can also mean something more substantial, and this is called 'deep framing'. 'Deep framing' refers to the connections that are forged between a particular communication strategy or public policy and a set of deeper values or principles,[15] and offers one method of linking climate change engagement strategies with self-transcendent values.[16] For example, putting a financial value on an endangered species, and building an economic case for their conservation, makes them equivalent (at the level of deep frames) to other 'assets' of the same value (like a hotel chain). This is a very different frame to one that attempts to achieve the same conservation goals through emphasising the intrinsic value of rare animal species, as something that should be protected in their own right.

Looking beyond sustainable behaviour, the animal rights charity PETA is notorious for its adverts which promote vegetarianism (but do so through images of scantily clad women). Critics say that they are doing more harm than good, by promoting misogynistic values. So it is clear that a message can cause 'collateral damage', even if it doesn't intend to.

Putting the theory into practice

Everyone has both self-enhancing and self-transcending values (we have all, at some point, treasured a material possession – but we have also all valued the health of a family member). People who promote sustainability do not (and should not) seek to try and 'change' people's values. But instead of stoking up self-interest, campaigns for sustainable behaviour can instead nurture and strengthen self-transcending values.

Certainly, this means 'meeting people where they are' as much as possible. Depending on your audience, different messages and ways of approaching the problem are appropriate. But there are limits on how far the meaning of a message about sustainable behaviour can be bent before it becomes broken and meaningless. Some things (regular flying or eating imported red meat everyday) are simply unsustainable, and pretending otherwise is in no-one's best interest.

> *The trick is to develop and apply 'bridges' between what you want to say (the message about sustainability) and the issues that your audience are interested in, but without inadvertently promoting values that make sustainable behaviours less achievable in the longer term.*

The bridges that can link your message and your audience are probably best identified by exploring the issue you want to address with a few people, and getting a sense of what might motivate them to change their behaviour.

Case study

A recent report called 'Common Cause', written for charitable organisations who frequently design campaigns to reach large numbers of people, applies the 'values and frames' thinking to a number of practical issues. The central argument of the Common Cause report is that for 'bigger-than-self' problems like climate change (i.e. problems that may not be in an individual's immediate self-interest to invest energy and resources in helping to solve), campaigns that propagate or endorse self-enhancing values may actually undermine the 'common cause' that links them.

Although this report was aimed at charities, its lessons can equally be applied to strategies for promoting sustainable behaviour. There is no point in undermining the argument that tackling climate change through sustainable behaviour is a shared challenge by focusing on the ways that sustainable behaviour may serve people's self-interest. This is undoubtedly an effective way of getting a single, well-defined behavioural change achieved – but at what cost?

Find out more

www.valuesandframes.org: the go-to resource for the latest thinking on using the right values and frames for sustainability.

http://www.wastewatch.org.uk/: an organisation which has been carefully applying these kinds of insights to their work with good practical examples.

....

CHAPTER 3

Harnessing The Power Of Social Norms

What you need to know

IT IS VERY RARE THAT PEOPLE ACT purely as individuals. We are social creatures, and we take a lot of our cues about how to behave from those around us, whether this is family, friends, colleagues or even strangers on the commute to work. Many strategies for promoting sustainable behaviour seem to forget this and focus exclusively on people as individuals.

This means that they are working against the grain of human nature and making the challenge of sustainability feel more overwhelming than it actually is. But by paying attention to social norms (the standards that we use to judge the appropriateness of our own behaviour), a much stronger sense of collective momentum can be generated, making any programme to promote sustainable behaviour much more likely to succeed.

The basic idea is that people tend to act in a way that is socially acceptable, and so if a particular behaviour (littering, for example, or driving a car with a large engine) can be cast in a socially unacceptable light, then people should be less likely to engage in it.

> *No-one likes to feel like they are acting in a way that their friends or colleagues don't approve of. So communicating the idea that sustainable behaviour is 'the norm' is a powerful tool.*

Pictures and videos of ordinary people ('like me') engaging in sustainable behaviours are a simple and effective way of generating a sense of social normality around saving energy.[17] Encouraging people to make public commitments (for example, signing up to make a specific change to their behaviour on a shared notice board) is another simple way of making 'private' behaviours 'public'. And studies have shown that when hotel guests are provided with information that other guests are re-using their towels, they are more likely to do this as well, over and above the impact of telling them about the environmental benefits.[18]

> *However, there is a danger that strategies based on social norms can backfire if they accidentally communicate the fact that lots of people are engaging in unsustainable behaviour.*

For example, a campaign focusing on the fact that too many people take internal flights actually contains two messages: that taking internal flights is bad for the environment and that lots of people are taking internal flights. This second message can make the campaign counterproductive: by conveying how common internal flights are, it can give those who do not currently take short-haul flights a perverse incentive to do so.

So use social norms carefully, and consider what information people will take from them. It is crucial to focus not only on what people are doing, but also on what they should be doing.

If you only do one thing...

Everyone has a peer group and a social network. Before you begin any campaign to promote sustainable behaviour, ask yourself who this group is for the people you are targeting, and try to ensure that your initiative has a social visibility, and is not simply restricted to personal emails or leaflets in people's pigeon holes. More than any information or facts you can give them, your audience will take their cues as to whether sustainable behaviour is something weird or something normal from their social group.

The theory that makes it work

Social norms are a powerful and effective way of influencing sustainable behaviours, but there are some pitfalls to avoid. As Robert Cialdini and his colleagues at Arizona State University have demonstrated repeatedly, the problem with appeals based on social norms is that they often contain a hidden message.[18] So, for example, in an experiment led by the psychologist Wesley Schultz,[17] researchers examined the influence of social norms on the household energy consumption of residents of California. The researchers picked houses at random and then divided them into groups depending on whether their energy consumption was higher or lower than the average for that area. Some low energy-use households received only information about average energy usage, thereby setting the social norm. A second group of low-energy households had a positive 'emoticon' (happy face) positioned next to their personal energy figure, conveying approval of their energy footprint. A third group of over-consuming households were shown their energy usage coupled with a negative emoticon (sad face), intended to convey disapproval of their higher-than-average footprint.

31

The researchers then measured energy consumption in the following months. As one might expect, the over-consuming households used the social norm as a motivation to reduce their energy use, but the under-consuming households that had received only the social norm information increased their energy use. Crucially though, the under-consuming households that had received positive feedback did not show this boomerang effect: the addition of a 'smiley face' next to their energy usage made all the difference. Despite the simplicity of the feedback, households that felt their under-consumption was socially approved (rather than a reason to relax) and maintained their small energy footprint. This suggests that using social norms can be effective, but only if they are used in the right way.

There are other ways of using social norms that don't rely on pointing to a 'silent majority' who are already engaging in a particular behaviour (because for many sustainable behaviours, positive norms are simply not there to promote). The Wasting Water is Weird (**http://wastingwaterisweird.com**) campaign uses a series of short videos to position wasting water as something only 'weird' people do. In the videos, a creepy, menacing character called Rip enthuses about wasting water, while someone 'ordinary' wastes water by, for example, leaving the tap on while brushing their teeth. The obvious implication is that if you waste water you are as socially undesirable as Rip.

In this campaign, social norms are being deployed to make a 'bad' behaviour appear to be the choice of a minority, neatly getting around the problem of no obvious 'good' social norms being readily available. But there is a risk with this type of approach, too: if the majority of people viewing the advert identify with the ordinary character, they may feel castigated and demonised for something that everyone else seems to view as normal.

Putting the theory into practice

Social norms are a fantastic method of amplifying the influence of existing good behaviours, but they can't bring about these good behaviours on their own. This means that social norm approaches have to be combined with more direct strategies for promoting sustainable behaviour in order to be effective, such as breaking habits down into manageable chunks (Chapter 4), or developing a sense of environmental responsibility that goes beyond individual behaviours (Chapter 2).

> *First, the right norms need to be created, then the power of social norm strategies can be fully realised.*

There are different reasons that people adopt social norms, and encouraging people to adopt a sustainable behaviour simply to 'conform', to avoid a feeling of guilt, or for fear of not 'fitting in', can lead to problems. Unfortunately, as the growing amount of 'greenwash' shows, the idea of sustainability can be a remarkably effective way of shifting patently unsustainable products.

We may currently compete through demonstrations of conspicuous material consumption, but material goods are simply a marker for social status. It's the social status that's important, and the markers we use to signify it can easily change.

> *We have a natural desire to try to out-do each other, and we will compete on whatever criteria happen to be around. But if people are only going green 'to be seen', then their level of engagement with the broader issue of sustainability is likely to be fairly shallow.*

If the use of social norms can be combined with an appeal to people's 'intrinsic' motivations (e.g. a sense of social belonging – see Chapter 2), they are likely to be more effective and persistent.

Case study

Academic research on social norms is now being put into practice by the energy company Opower, who have achieved small but consistent savings on average energy use with their US customers.[19] Opower's approach is deceptively simple: every customer who receives an energy bill also receives information about how much energy they are using relative to their neighbours. The energy bills that Opower customers receive show average usage relative to immediate neighbours ('people like them'), give feedback about recent bills (through positive or negative emoticons) and contain tips for saving energy.

Opower is are now trialling similar techniques in the UK. The hope is that when combined with improvements to household insulation made possible through the government's 'green deal', and 'smart' energy meters that can monitor not only household-level use, but room-by-room and appliance-by-appliance, significant reductions in energy use will be achieved.

Find out more

Find out more about Opower's use of social norms
for reducing energy bills
(http://opower.com/what-is-opower/reports/)

....

CHAPTER 4

Breaking Bad Habits and Creating Good Ones

What you need to know

HOW DOES YOUR AVERAGE DAY START? More than likely with a bleary-eyed stampede to get out of the house and into work, most of which is done on auto-pilot. For a species that prides itself on its unique consciousness, we do an awful lot of things without much conscious awareness.

> *Habits – good and bad – define us, and un-sustainable behaviour is often a product of un-conscious thought processes.*

A huge amount of household energy use is embedded in habitual behaviours. This is one of the reasons that despite good intentions we often fail to make changes that would reduce the amount of energy we use. We know that we *could* get the bus to work, but something always gets in the way (no umbrella for the walk to the bus stop or an out-of-date timetable). We know that re-using shopping bags is a small and simple way to reduce waste, but somehow, we only remember this once we arrive at the shop. We are not used to thinking through the energy-use implications of our behaviours, but we can if we need to, and there is a reliable body of research that shows how.

> *The problem is that something seemingly straightforward like getting the bus to work is actually made up of lots of smaller (habitual) decisions, all of which can derail even the best intentions.*

One strategy for dealing with this challenge that has been developed over a number of years by studying how habits form (and how they change), involves breaking habitual behaviours down into 'if...then' style plans.

Driving to work might not seem like a 'habit', but break down what needs to happen to change this behaviour and it soon becomes clear that there is a lot of non-conscious decision-making going on beneath the surface. Most of the barriers to changing a behaviour can only be addressed by getting down to a level of detail that doesn't come naturally to most of us. And even though some of the steps might seem trivial, it is exactly these sorts of minor details that can wreck the best-laid plans.

Research has shown that forming even very strong *overall* goal intentions (without breaking the behaviour down into smaller chunks) leaves a large gap between intention and action. In particular, people can fail to get started (because there is no specified starting point) and can get derailed along the way (because there are not enough markers of progress).

Periods of *transition*, where routines are already in flux, provide useful opportunities to develop new, more sustainable habits. In the context of home insulation, some building work already scheduled for the house might provide not only the practical opportunity for some low-carbon upgrades, but also the perfect chance for making some long-intended changes to habits and routines.

Campaigns and initiatives based on these strategies have a proven track for behaviours as diverse as driving, recycling and increasing purchases of organic food.

> *The bottom line is that breaking behaviours down into small parts helps to bridge the infamous gap between good intentions and achieving outcomes, making planned changes in behaviour more likely to be realised.*

If you only do one thing...

Pick a high-impact sustainable behaviour from Box 1 in Chapter 1 that you think it is possible to have an impact on, and break it down into its most basic components. For each component, make an 'if...then' plan to ensure that achieving your overall goal is not obstructed by a hidden, habitual component of the behaviour.

The theory that makes it work

The basic idea behind changing bad habits and creating good ones is that any habitual behaviour can be broken down into sets of *intended* actions that are *implemented* as part of an overall goal. Breaking habits down into distinct *'implementation intentions'* allows not only the constituent parts of a certain behaviour to be identified, but also the barriers that might prevent *changing* that behaviour.[20]

To form an implementation intention, a person must first identify a response that is important for goal attainment and, second, anticipate a critical cue to initiate that response. For example, a person might specify a behaviour ('choose healthy option from menu'), and a situational cue with which to trigger it ('when I am reading the menu outside of the restaurant'). Making a detailed plan like this, which is contingent on situational cues, allows changes to be made if necessary – in this case, because the menu has been checked for healthy options before entering the restaurant, the diner can choose to move on if there are no healthy options on the menu (rather than be forced to choose an unhealthy option once seated). However, while they allow flexibility, they also tap into 'good' habits and the person does not need to think or deliberate too much about what to do next: there are specific 'if-then' rules to guide the way.

Implementation intentions have been used to successfully influence behaviour relating to driving behaviour,[21] consumer habits,[22] workplace recycling[23] and increasing the amount that people use public transport and buy organic food.[24] The strategy used in the study to encourage people to use buses more frequently was very simple: some people were asked to make a specific plan including a day and time for taking a new bus route to their university, whereas others were just asked to commit to using the bus more (at some point). Adding a financial incentive did not have any additional impact over and above making a step-by-step plan.

Putting the theory into practice

A central theme of this book is that although sustainable behaviour in general is important, focusing too much on *single* behaviours – particularly if they have only a limited impact in terms of energy saved – can be problematic. However, sometimes it makes sense to pick a behaviour (or related set of behaviours) to focus on, and these examples give an idea of the habitual components hiding within seemingly straightforward behaviours.

BOX 2

Example A: Getting the bus to work, instead of driving

Overall goal: Get the bus to work on Thursdays and Fridays

Breaking down the goal:

IF... it is Wednesday or Thursday evening, *THEN* set the alarm clock early enough to allow extra time to get to work.

IF it is Wednesday or Thursday evening, *THEN* have a shower to save time in morning.

IF there is a walk to the bus stop, *THEN* leave an umbrella by the door in case it rains.

Example B: Improving home insulation

Improving home insulation could involve any number of changes, but it is too late once the winter comes round again and the heating is cranked up for another year.

Overall goal: To improve insulation in home

Breaking down the goal:

IF it is dusk, *THEN* close all the curtains in your house.

IF there is a draft coming under door, *THEN* write a note to buy a draft excluder on the weekend, and stick it on your notice board.

IF it is cold near to external doors, *THEN* fill unused keyholes with tissue paper.

Case study

One of the areas of sustainable behaviour that this kind of approach is most applicable to is travel behaviour and several campaigns have shown that focusing on the detail of complex goals like 'using public transport more often' is an effective way of achieving real results.

A few years ago in Australia, the government developed a programme called 'Travelsmart'. Thousands of people took part in the Travelsmart programme, and cut their carbon emissions by nearly 15%.

The programme worked so well because everyone who took part was provided with their own individualised travel plan.

This approach has since been taken up and adopted by the British Sustainable Transport charity Sustrans. Their work involves visiting people at home, reaching people at schools of in the workplace, and identifying exactly what their individual barriers and challenges to travelling more sustainably are. They then provide simple, motivating tools such as personalised maps, bus routes and information on safe walking and cycling paths.

An evaluation of 14 personalised travel plan initiatives across the UK found significant changes in travel behaviour, with an estimated saving of approximately 11.4 million car km a year.

Find out more

An evaluation of Sustrans's personalised travel plan initiatives
(http://www.sustrans.org.uk/assets/files/travelsmart/
dft_susttravel_pdf_040054.pdf)

Using planning to create new recycling habits at work
(http://www.goallab.nl/publications/documents/
Holland,%20Aarts,%20Langendam%20%282006%29%20-%20
implementation%20intentions%20on%20the%20workfloor.pdf)

CHAPTER 5

Using Scare Tactics: Does It Work?

What you need to know

CLIMATE CHANGE – AND THE CHALLENGE of getting to grips with sustainability – can seem daunting. But a lot of attempts at promoting sustainable behaviour fail because they simply make people feel guilty and don't inspire action. In a nutshell, studies on using fear (e.g. images of burning globes or starving children, or apocalyptic messages about destruction and despair) to motivate sustainable behaviour show that this approach has the potential to change attitudes towards the environment (for example, expressions of concern), but often not people's actions.

While fear of a negative outcome (e.g. lung cancer) can be an effective way of promoting behavioural changes (e.g. giving up smoking), the link between the threat and the behaviour must be personal and direct.

For most people in wealthy countries like the UK, climate change is perceived as neither a direct nor a personal threat and so shocking people into doing their recycling is not necessarily the right idea.

One piece of research found that images that induced fear (such as environmental refugees or 'drowning' polar bears) were good for attracting attention, but ineffective at motivating genuine personal engagement (i.e. doing something about it!). Scaring people can work as a kind of 'spark' to generate awareness, but this must be coupled with constructive, practical information and support so that people can do something about it.

Un-threatening images that relate to people's everyday actions and concerns are more effective, and this links directly to work on using 'social norms' to promote sustainable behaviour (see Chapter 3). Showing people pictures of other people ('like them') engaging in meaningful sustainable behaviours (rather than scaring them with apocalyptic images) is likely to be a more productive way of motivating sustainable behaviour.

> *People need to know that other folk have also recognised the risks of climate change and that they are doing something about it.*

Another good strategy is to try and reduce the 'psychological distance' between people and climate change. Increased flooding is one of the impacts that scientists are very confident the UK will experience. Some research has looked, therefore, at the link between people's perceptions of climate change and whether or not they had suffered from flooding before. A study at Cardiff University[25] found that people who had experienced a flooding event were more likely to express concern over climate change and – crucially – to show a greater willingness to save energy to prevent the effects of climate change.

> *So linking individual experiences with climate change is one way of increasing the chance that people will want to do something about it.*

If you only do one thing...

If you want to raise awareness about the threat that the risks of climate change pose, try to do this using 'local' impacts. In the UK, there are a range of threats that climate change poses – none of them are catastrophic, but they are serious and people will be able to identify with them much more easily than talk of famine in sub-Saharan Africa. This short summary of how climate change will affect the UK (**http://webarchive. nationalarchives.gov.uk/20121015000000/www.direct.gov.uk/en/ Environmentandgreenerliving/Thewiderenvironment/Climatechange/ DG_072929**) may be useful. But don't just raise awareness of the risk – use the information in this book to explain concrete steps for doing something about it.

The theory that makes it work

For people who live in developed countries, climate change is mostly an 'invisible' threat, something that happens not here and not now. Although a changing climate will cause a range of problems for the UK – especially increased flooding and all the risks associated with it – it is difficult to point to locally relevant images or statistics that really capture the scale of the problem (at least for now). So, in order to show people in countries like the UK how bad climate change will be unless we move towards a more sustainable society, many early attempts at engaging the public by environmental charities or government agencies focused on finding ways of increasing the 'fear factor'. With pictures of starving African children, burning globes and drowning polar bears, the stereotypical imagery of climate change communication was born.

But research has now established that these images are not great ways of communicating climate change. For those who do not yet realise the potentially 'scary' aspects of climate change, people need to first experience themselves as vulnerable to the risks in some way in order to feel moved or affected.[25,26,27] The danger is that fear-inducing images and messages can be disempowering, producing feelings of helplessness, remoteness and lack of control.[28]

Unless carefully used in a message that contains constructive advice and a personal and direct link with the individual, fear is likely to trigger barriers to engagement with climate change, such as denial.[29,30] Similarly, studies have shown that guilt can play a role in motivating people to take action but can also function to stimulate defensive mechanisms against the perceived threat or challenge to people's sense of identity (as a good, moral person).

In fact, a study by psychologists at Berkeley, California[31] found that 'apocalyptic' messages about climate change impacted on different people in different ways. For those who believed in a 'just world' – that bad things don't, by and large, happen to good people – messages that ended in dire consequences actually increased their scepticism about climate change. The researchers suggested that the conflict between the negative impacts of climate change (happening to 'good people') and their belief in a just world led to the message being ignored, and even used as evidence that climate change was not occurring.

Putting the theory into practice

If you can identify a 'local' risk of climate change, and identify practical steps people can take to reduce that risk, then you will be using the threat of climate change in the way that is most likely to lead to behaviour change.

However, it is difficult to point to any definitive impacts of climate change that have *already* occurred. Increased flooding is one of the climate change impacts that the UK will have to face, but of course flooding happened before humans started to alter the climate.

So be careful not to overstate the link between climate change and extreme weather events like flooding. You can say that climate change makes these kinds of occurrences more likely to happen – it loads the dice – but it is not, on its own, responsible for every flood or heat wave that take place.

Case study

In 2009, the UK government launched a TV advertisement and series of newspaper adverts named 'Bedtime Stories', which were designed to engage the public on climate change. The TV advert depicted a young girl being read a scary story about climate change as cartoon sea levels rose around her house and spooky music played in the background. The story in the ad rather dramatically suggested that it was possible to 'save the land for the children' and showed a cartoon girl turning off her bedroom light, ending with the message: 'it's up to us how the story ends... see what you can do: search online for "ActOn CO2"'. The campaign was withdrawn following complaints to the Advertising Standards Authority about the newspaper ads, which were judged to have made too strong a link between flooding and climate change. But many people also criticised the TV advert on the basis that using scare tactics was not an especially good way of encouraging sustainable behaviour.

So what should it have said instead? The basic concept of a children's story is not necessarily a bad one, but as most people do not feel personally threatened by climate change, going for the scare tactics was not a good decision. Instead, the story could have focused on characters who worked together to share the challenge of creating a more sustainable society, presented images of ordinary, everyday people cycling to work, taking the train to go on holiday, or discussing ways of making their houses more heat-efficient with their neighbours.

Find out more

Avoid the Bedtime Stories approach
(http://www.youtube.com/watch? v=SDthR9RHOgw)

CHAPTER 6

Putting It All Together: Making Wider Change

THIS SHORT BOOK IS DESIGNED to provide practical – but crucially, evidence-based – guidance for promoting sustainable behaviour. By focusing on high-impact behaviours (Chapter 1), thinking about the values and sense of identity that underpin individual actions (Chapter 2), paying attention to the powerful influence of social norms and social networks (Chapter 3), using well-targeted strategies for breaking complex, habitual behaviours down into manageable chunks (Chapter 4) and avoiding the scare tactics and guilt-trips of so many environmental campaigns (Chapter 5), it is possible to design programmes for promoting sustainable behaviour that are meaningful, effective and have a measurable impact.

Following these principles will also provide the best chance of sustaining change over time. If a behaviour becomes defining for an individual (or even better their social group); if new, sustainable habits can be created; and if the sorts of values that go hand-in-hand with sustainable behaviour can be activated and nurtured, then sustainable behaviours won't simply disappear as soon as the financial incentive isn't there, or the initial interest subsides.

But even the best-designed campaign to promote sustainable behaviour is limited in its scope if it fails to link everyday behaviours to the wider challenges of sustainability. How can bridges between individual-level changes and community/social/political processes be made? What are the factors beyond behaviour change that anyone promoting sustainability should always have in the back of their mind? How does sustainable behaviour fit into the bigger picture?

Social networks

Chapter 3 began to answer the question of how to go beyond thinking about people as isolated individuals and harness the power of social norms. But the strategy of focusing on the 'social' rather than the 'individual' can be taken much further than asking people to make visible public commitments (e.g. a pledge on a car-share notice board), or spreading positive social norms by providing people with information about what their colleagues are doing.

> *Social networks (real, physical ones as well as online commun-ities) are everywhere, and new behaviours spread through social networks like the ripples of a stone dropped into a pond.*

Most people do not have a social network with sustainability at its core, but working to develop a group – rather than individual – sense of environmental responsibility and identity should be at the heart of any sustainability campaign. What is it that defines the group you are targeting and how can this identity be linked to sustainable behaviour?

The extent to which new behaviours spread though a social network depends on the number of 'social ties', but also on the strength of those ties.[32] Information is likely to spread quickly the more 'ties' there are in a network, but it is more likely to influence behaviour when it is received through strong ties (for example, a family member) than weak ones. So think about who is involved in promoting sustainable behaviour – is it a well-liked colleague with lots of strong social ties at work?

The idea that information and innovation can spread through social networks is not a new one. In the field of commercial marketing, advertising campaigns targeting 'opinion leaders' and influential individuals is commonplace. In other fields – health behaviour, for example – campaigns often target peer groups and existing social networks, in the hope that the spreading of positive health behaviours will be more likely within groups of individuals who trust each other and pay attention to each others' behaviour.

Targeting social networks also helps to enhance 'social capital' – something that is critical for building the resilience to cope with and adapt to changes brought about by adapting to climate change.[33] And the effectiveness of group-based programmes at promoting pro-environmental behaviour change has been demonstrated on numerous occasions – participants in these projects consistently point to a sense of mutual learning and support as a key reason for making and maintaining changes in behaviour.[34]

Social networks are important for creating a social identity that incorporates sustainability as a guiding principle,[35] rather than simply passing on a series of disjointed behaviours that may benefit the environment. If sustainable behaviour becomes *defining* for a social group, more significant behavioural changes (reinforced through peer pressure) are likely to be forthcoming.

Employers – reciprocal change

If you are promoting sustainable behaviour at work, then there is an obvious place that most workers would look to for leadership: their employer.

> *Changes in personal behaviour among workers can catalyse further changes from an employer because the argument that 'we've done our bit, now you do yours' is a powerful one.*

Also, if campaigns to promote sustainable behaviour are framed around the right kinds of values, they can help to generate a different type of workplace culture, one where it is normal to work co-operatively with others on issues like climate change and sustainability. However, while working co-operatively to reduce the carbon footprint of the organisation as a whole is clearly a must, there is nothing to say that a bit of friendly competition hurts either, as this example (**http://www.cloudapps.com/**) of a work-based sustainability tool shows.

Developed by a firm called CloudApps, the sustainability measuring and reporting system allows groups of colleagues to record their carbon use, and compete to see who can save the most energy. Drawing directly on research showing the importance of social norms and social networks for promoting sustainable behaviour, firms that have adopted the tool have shown considerable energy savings.

> *By taking advantage of the natural human desire to keep up with the Joneses, applications like this can kick-start a process of change that has a momentum all of its own.*

Many employers run formal car-share schemes, but if this is not yet in place where you work, then consider following a guide like **one** from **www.liftshare.com** and setting one up. Although it is written with employers in mind, it contains loads of useful tools for getting employers interested. It includes surveys that you (or your employer) can give to members of staff to gauge interest, as well as useful examples of what incentives other employers have offered to staff signing up to car share schemes at work (although remember that incentives should be linked to 'intrinsic' values as much as possible). But even if your employer won't go as far as establishing a formal car-share scheme, they may be able to provide incentives such as priority parking spaces for car-sharers.

> *Always consider how practical steps like these can be as well-informed as possible by the research evidence: foster positive social norms, break complex behaviours down into manageable chunks, and frame your messages around values that will catalyse more sustainable behaviours in the future.*

The Cycle to Work scheme is a national initiative run by the UK government, aimed at providing employees with tax-free bikes. Typical savings are between 30 and 50% of the price of a new bike. Employers can run the scheme themselves, or sign up with a third-party provider such as **www.cyclescheme.co.uk**. Employees then visit an approved bike shop, choose their bike and accessories, and arrange for the cost to be invoiced to the employer. The employee then 'hires' the bike from the employer through regular monthly instalments, until the bike is paid for, at which point they make a final payment and take permanent ownership of the bike.

The link between personal change and political change

There is a circular relationship between public views and the policies that politicians think are acceptable to support. Without the backing of the public, ambitious changes to the way our energy is supplied, or our transport system is structured, will never happen. But public views are to some extent shaped by the urgency with which the government and the media treat an issue. If politicians go quiet on climate change and sustainability, this sends a powerful signal that it is not a top priority.

So any campaign to promote sustainable behaviour in the workplace should try to make an explicit link between ordinary, everyday behaviours and government strategies for sustainability. One obvious way of doing this is to support Trade Union initiatives for 'green jobs', which argue that especially during tough economic times, investment in low-carbon employment is critical.

> *It is critical to ensure that focusing on individual behaviour changes does not become a diversion from the process of bringing political pressure to bear on policy-makers, and the importance of public demonstrations of frustration at both the lack of political progress on sustainability and the barriers presented by vested interests should not be underestimated.*

There is no reason that developing messages about sustainable behaviour should be detached from the political context, and communicating about sustainability can play a role in fostering demand for – as well as acceptance of – policy change.[36]

Focusing on sustainable behaviour in the workplace is also a very good way of identifying all the structural barriers to behaviour change, such as the cost of public transport or the lack of safe cycling lanes. These are not issues that any one individual – or even an entire organisation – could do much about. But if a group of people can show that they have done everything within their power to move towards sustainability, and there are still barriers in the way, then this is a powerful argument to persuade local and national policy-makers to take action.

However, there is one more important reason why promoting sustainable behaviour should never be detached from the politics of sustainability. How people act says something about their underlying values, the priorities they hold, and the type of world they want to live in. It may have become a tired old cliché, but 'being the change you want to see' still sends out an important message. If done right, promoting sustainable behaviour can mean so much more than a clever slogan or an appeal for people to 'do their bit' – it can be a political act in itself.

Conclusion

THE IDEA THAT WE NEED TO WORK towards a more sustainable society is no longer a fringe position. It is only going to become more important over the coming years and decades. Promoting sustainable behaviour is not easy, but armed with the best evidence and practical advice it is possible to make meaningful, measurable, and long-lasting changes in people's behaviour at home and in the workplace.

> *If there is one message to take away from this book, it is that individuals – and individual behaviours – cannot be separated from their social context.*

We act according to our personal values and priorities and in line with the social norms of our peer group, whereupon much of our everyday behaviour becomes habitual and difficult to change. Focus on linking specific behaviours with underlying values, understand that people look to others around them for cues about what to do, and try not to become too bogged down with actions that have a limited payoff in terms of sustainability.

The social science research presented in this book gives you signposts and educated guidance, but because humans are not machines, it doesn't give you guarantees. It tells you how people *tend* to behave and respond, but there is no substitute for having an in-depth understanding of the audience you are working with. So this book provides you – the catalyst

CONCLUSION

for change – with the tools you need, not the finished product. It may seem an uphill struggle at times. But there is a critical role for people's everyday behaviour to play in the transition towards sustainability.

....

Mapping Principles to Case Studies

Principle for promoting sustainable behaviour	Where is this being applied
Focus on 'intrinsic' values	The website **www.valuesandframes.org** shows how organisations from the private, public and charity sectors are framing their messages about sustainability using values that make a sustainable society more likely in the long run.
Harness the power of social norms	The energy company Opower (**www.opower. com**) is transforming the way people receive their energy bills by applying the latest thinking on social norms.
Create sustainable habits	Before you can change a habit, you need to break it down into bite-size chunks. Sustrans's (**www.sustrans.org.uk**) 'Travelsmart' programme identifies individual barriers and challenges to travelling more sustainably and provides simple, motivating tools such as personalised maps, bus routes and information on safe walking and cycling paths.

Avoid scare tactics	Learn from the government's mistakes. Watch the Bedtime Stories advert (**http://www.youtube.com/watch? v=SDthR9RHOgw**), and don't promote your campaign for sustainable behaviour by showing scared kids and cartoon floods.
Tap into social competition in the workplace	The success of the CloudApps (**www.cloudapps.com**) software in some big organisations shows that tapping into social norms and social networks – and the natural competitiveness that we all possess – can lead to big carbon savings.

Promoting Sustainable Behaviour – The People and Projects That You Need to Know About

THERE ARE NOW SEVERAL GROUPS and organisations doing good work on sustainable behaviour, as well as some excellent online resources. The 'Green Living' blog (http://greenallianceblog.org.uk/category/behaviour-change/), an initiative of Green Alliance (http://www.green-alliance.org.uk/home/), is a good place to explore in more depth debates about how best to promote sustainable behaviour. The website 'Talking Climate' (http://www.talkingclimate.org, edited by the author of this book) offers a gateway to new research on climate change communication, and regular blogs from leading academics in the field.

In terms of practical projects, there are several third-sector organisations which do good work on sustainable behaviour. Sustrans (http://www.sustrans.org.uk) is a charity that focuses on promoting more sustainable transport behaviour, using evidence from research studies to inform its programmes, while the charity Global Action Plan (http://www.globalactionplan.org.uk/) describes itself as the UK's 'leading environmental behaviour change charity', and has initiated and led lots of projects aimed at generating lasting behavioural changes in community and work-based groups.

Although different political parties have different ideas about whether they 'do' behaviour change or not, the current government houses a Behavioural Insights Team (**http://www.cabinetoffice.gov.uk/behavioural-insights-team**), which has produced a report on behaviour change and energy use. Under new legislation launched in 2012 (known as the 'Green Deal' – **http://www.decc.gov.uk/en/content/cms/tackling/green_deal/green_deal.aspx**), the government is aiming to install insulation in 14 million households by 2020, and provide millions of 'smart meters' that will help people monitor their energy use. The success of the Green Deal will hinge on whether people buy into it and so this is a huge opportunity for incorporating evidence on how to promote sustainable behaviour effectively.

....

References

1. Druckman, A., Chitnisa, M., Sorrell, S. and Jackson, T. 2011. Missing carbon reductions? Exploring rebound and backfire effects in UK households. *Energy Policy* (Volume 39): 3572–3581.

2. Vlek, C., Rothengatter, T., Steg, L. and Abrahamse, W. 2005. A review of intervention studies aimed at household energy conservation. *Journal of Environmental Psychology* (Volume 25 Issue 3): 273–291.

3. Thøgersen, J. and Crompton, T. 2009. Simple and painless? The limitations of spillover in environmental campaigning. *Journal of Consumer Policy* (Volume 32): 141–163.

4. Spence, A. and Pidgeon, N.F. 2009. Psychology, climate change and sustainable behavior. *Environment: Science and Policy for Sustainable Development* (Volume 6): 8–18.

5. Berners-Lee, M. 2010. *How Bad are Bananas? The Carbon Footprint of Everything* (London: Profile Books Ltd).

6. Gardner, G. and Stern, P. 2009. The short list: The most effective actions U.S. households can take to curb climate change. *Environment*, December, 2009.

7. Schwartz, S.H. 1992. Universals in the content and structure of values: Theoretical advances and empirical tests in 20 countries. In: Zanna, M.P. (Ed.) *Advances in Experimental Social Psychology*, vol. 25 (San Diego, CA: Academic Press), pp. 1– 65.

8. Stern, P.C. 2000. Towards a coherent theory of environmentally significant behavior. *Journal of Social Issues* (Volume 56): 407–424.

9. Slimak, M.W. and Dietz, T. 2006. Personal values, beliefs, and ecological risk perception. *Risk Analysis* (Volume 26): 1689–1705.

REFERENCES

10. Dunlap, R.E., Grieneeks, J.K. and Rokeach, M., 1983. Human values and pro-environmental behaviour. In: Conn, W.D. (Ed.) *Energy and Material Resources: Attitudes, Values, and Public Policy* (Boulder, CO: Westview Press).

11. Nilsson, A., von Borgstede, C. and Biel, A. 2004. Willingness to accept climate change strategies: The effect of values and norms. *Journal of Environmental Psychology* (Volume 24): 267–277.

12. Dobson, A. 2010. *Environmental Citizenship and Pro-environmental Behaviour: Rapid Research and Evidence Review* (London: Sustainable Development Research Network).

13. Whitmarsh, L. and O'Neill, S. 2010. Green identity, green living? The role of pro-environmental self-identity in determining consistency across diverse pro-environmental behaviours. *Journal of Environmental Psychology* (Volume 30): 305–314.

14. Evans, L., Maio, G., Corner, A., Hodgetts, C.J., Ahmed, S. and Hahn, U. 2012. Self interest and pro-environmental behaviour. *Nature Climate Change*. doi: 10.1038/NCLIMATE1662.

15. Lakoff, G., 2004. *Don't Think of an Elephant! Know Your Values and Frame the Debate* (White River Junction, VT: Chelsea Green Publishing).

16. Crompton, T. 2010. *Common Cause: The Case for Working with Our Cultural Values* (Godalming, Surrey: WWF UK).

17. Schultz, P.W., Nolan, J.M., Cialdini, R.B., Goldstein, N.J. and Griskevicius, V. 2007. The constructive, destructive, and reconstructive power of social norms. *Psychological Science* (Volume 18 Issue 5): 429–434.

18. Cialdini, R.B. 2003. Crafting normative messages to protect the environment. *Current Directions in Psychological Science* (Volume 12 Issue 4): 105–109.

19. Allcott, H. 2011. Social norms and energy conservation. *Journal of Public Economics* (Volume 95, 1082–1095).

20. Gollwitzer, P.M. 1999. Implementation intentions: Strong effects of simple plans. *American Psychologist* (Volume 54): 493–503.

21. Elliot, M.A. and Armitage, C.J. 2006. Effects of implementations on the self-reported frequency of drivers' compliance with speed limits. *Journal of Experimental Psychology: Applied* (Volume 12): 108–117.

22. Verplanken, B. and Wood, W. 2006. Interventions to break and create consumer habits. *Journal of Public Policy and Marketing* (Volume 25): 90–103.

23. Holland, R.W., Aarts, H. and Langendam, D. 2006. Breaking and creating habits on the working floor: A field-experiment on the power of implementation intentions. *Journal of Experimental Social Psychology* (Volume 42): 776–783.

24. Bamberg, S. 2002. Effects of implementation intentions on the actual performance of new environmentally friendly behaviours – results of two field experiments. *Journal of Environmental Psychology* (Volume 22): 399–411.

25. Spence, A., Poortinga, W., Butler, C. and Pidgeon, N. 2011. Perceptions of climate change and willingness to save energy related to flood experience. *Nature Climate Change* (Volume 1 Issue 1): 46–49.

26. Das, E.H.H.J., de Wit, J.B.F. and Stroebe, W. 2003. Fear appeals motivate acceptance of action recommendations: Evidence for a positive bias in the processing of persuasive messages. *Personality and Social Psychology Bulletin* (Volume 29): 650–664

27. Hoog, N., Stroebe, W. and de Wit, J.B.F. 2005. The impact of fear appeals on processing and acceptance of action recommendations. *Personality & Social Psychology Bulletin* (Volume 31): 24–33.

28. O'Neill, S. and Nicholson-Cole, S. 2009. 'Fear won't do it': Promoting positive engagement with climate change through visual and iconic representations. *Science Communication* (Volume 30): 355–379.

29. Stoll-Kleemann, S., O'Riordan, T. and Jaeger, C.C. 2001. The psychology of denial concerning climate mitigation measures: Evidence from Swiss focus groups. *Global Environmental Change* (Volume 11 Issue 2): 107–117.

30. Lorenzoni, I., Nicholson-Cole, S. and Whitmarsh, L. 2007. Barriers perceived to engaging with climate change among the UK public and their policy implications. *Global Environmental Change* (Volume 17 Issue 3–4): 445–459.

31. Feinberg, M. and Willer, R. 2010. Apocalypse soon? Dire messages reduce belief in global warming by contradicting just-world beliefs. *Psychological Science* (Volume 22 Issue 1): 34–38.

32. Granovetter, M.S. 1973. The strength of weak ties. *American Journal of Sociology* (Volume 78): 1360–1380.

33. Rowson, J., Broome, S. and Jones, A. 2010. *Connected Communities: How Social Networks Power and Sustain the Big Society* (London: Royal Society of Arts).

34. Nye, M. and Burgess, J. 2008. *Promoting Durable Change in Household Waste and Energy Use Behaviour* (London: Department for Environment, Food & Rural Affairs, UK).

35. Rabinovich, A., Morton, T.A. and Duke, C.C. 2010. Collective self and individual choice: The role of social comparisons in promoting climate change. In: Whitmarsh, L., O'Neill, S. and Lorenzoni, I. (Eds) *Engaging the Public with Climate Change: Behaviour Change and Communication* (London: Earthscan).

36. Ockwell, D., O'Neill, S. and Whitmarsh, L. 2009. Reorienting climate change communication for effective mitigation: Forcing people to be green or fostering grass-roots engagement? *Science Communication* (Volume 30): 305–327.

....

For Product Safety Concerns and Information please contact our EU
representative GPSR@taylorandfrancis.com
Taylor & Francis Verlag GmbH, Kaufingerstraße 24, 80331 München, Germany

www.ingramcontent.com/pod-product-compliance
Ingram Content Group UK Ltd.
Pitfield, Milton Keynes, MK11 3LW, UK
UKHW040927180425
457613UK00011B/281